Antaryātrā — The Inner Journey
An English Transliteration

A Collection of Hindi Poems by Anand Kumar Ashodhiya

English Translation by
Anand Kumar Ashodhiya

ISBN: 978-93-5626-749-7
First Edition: January 2026
Published: January 2026

Self-published by Anand Kumar Ashodhiya
under the imprint
Avikavani Publishers

Avikavani Publishers
Shahpur Turk, Sonipat, Haryana

Antaryātrā — The Inner Journey
An English Transliteration

A Collection of Hindi Poems by Anand Kumar Ashodhiya

English Translation by
Anand Kumar Ashodhiya

ISBN: 978-93-5626-749-7
First Edition: January 2026
Published: January 2026

Avikavani Publishers
Shahpur Turk · Sonipat · Haryana

2026

Copyright & Imprint Page

Antaryātrā — The Inner Journey
An English Transliteration

(A Collection of Hindi Poems by Anand Kumar Ashodhiya)

English Translation by
Anand Kumar Ashodhiya

First Edition Published: January 2026
ISBN: **978-93-5626-749-7**

Published by: Avikavani Publishers
Shahpur Turk, Sonipat, Haryana – 131001
Email: ashodhiya68@gmail.com

Table of Contents

FOREWORD

Dr. Puranmal Gaur
Former Director, Haryana Sahitya Akademi

Antaryātrā (The Inner Journey) is not merely a collection of poems by Anand Kumar Ashodhiya; it is a sustained moral and imaginative inquiry into the inner life of the individual as it stands in dialogue with society, history, and conscience. This is a poetry that does not hurry toward spectacle or proclamation. Instead, it listens—patiently, attentively—to the quieter urgencies of existence: memory, responsibility, longing, faith, dissent, and ethical choice.

The journey evoked here is inward, but never insular. Ashodhiya's poetic sensibility understands introspection not as withdrawal from the world, but as a deeper engagement with it. His poems arise from lived experience—personal, social, and cultural—and transform that experience into reflective utterance. Silence, in his work, is not emptiness but deliberation; emotion is not indulgence but discipline; devotion is not ritual alone, but moral attentiveness.

Linguistically, Ashodhiya's poetry carries the unmistakable fragrance of Haryana's soil—earth-bound, direct, and unpretentious—while remaining firmly rooted in the discipline of classical Hindi poetics. His diction moves with ease between the folk idiom and the philosophical register, allowing local experience to assume universal resonance. This balance between rootedness and reach is one of the defining strengths of his work.

Across the poems included in this volume, one encounters a wide emotional and ethical spectrum. In poems such as “Kade Aajya Yaad Teri,” longing is rendered through melody and restraint rather than excess. In “Laazmi Hai Ki Tu Maun Ho Ja,” silence becomes an ethical position—a necessary pause in an age of noise. In “Ration Depot Dhark Ki Aatmakatha,” the mundane mechanisms of everyday corruption are elevated into moral allegory, exposing how injustice operates not only through systems, but through habit and indifference.

What distinguishes Ashodhiya’s poetry is its triple essence: devotion, emotion, and dissent. His devotional poems are reflective rather than dogmatic; his love poems are intimate without sentimentality; his protest poems are forceful without rhetorical aggression. His patriotism emerges as a quiet responsibility toward collective memory and ethical inheritance, not as performative fervour. His social critique arises from empathy as much as from anger, grounded in realism and moral concern.

Certain recurring motifs—fire, thread, silence, eyes—move through this collection with symbolic consistency. These are not decorative images but conceptual emblems: fire that purifies as much as it burns; thread that binds while reminding one of impermanence; silence that speaks; sight that witnesses without exhibition. Together, they articulate a worldview marked by endurance, humility, and moral vigilance.

Ashodhiya's poetry reminds us that true literary expression is not born of display, but of sustained inward labour. His poems do not shout; they resonate. They do not instruct; they invite reflection. In an era increasingly shaped by immediacy and excess, Antaryātrā reclaims the quiet authority of the moral lyric—an authority once central to the finest traditions of Hindi poetry.

This book thus stands simultaneously as a personal pilgrimage and a social document—a bridge between individual conscience and collective experience. In Anand Kumar Ashodhiya's verses, one encounters not only a poet, but a witness, a reform-minded observer, and above all, a humanist committed to ethical clarity.

May Antaryātrā inspire readers not merely to admire poetry, but to undertake their own inward journeys—with attentiveness, courage, and compassion.

Dr. Puranmal Gaur
Former Director
Haryana Sahitya Akademi

PREFACE

Dr. Babu Ram (D.Litt.)
Head & Chairperson, Department of Hindi
Baba Mastnath University, Rohtak, Haryana

Poetry, before it assumes the shape of verse, exists as a condition of attentiveness. It is a heightened awareness of life's ordinary truths—those subtle tremors of thought and feeling that often pass unnoticed in the din of daily existence. In **Antaryātrā**, Anand Kumar Ashodhiya approaches poetry not as performance, nor as ornamentation of language, but as a disciplined inward practice: a way of listening to the self, the world, and the ethical tensions that bind them together.

This collection bears the marks of a poet who has learned to dwell patiently with experience. Ashodhiya's verses arise from lived moments—domestic, social, devotional, and philosophical—yet they are never confined to anecdote. Each poem moves from experience toward reflection, from emotion toward meaning. What emerges is not a display of sentiment, but a thoughtful shaping of consciousness into language.

Linguistically, **Antaryātrā** occupies a distinctive space within contemporary Hindi poetry. The poet's idiom is nourished by the cadences of Haryanvi speech—its directness, its moral clarity, its folk wisdom—yet it is tempered by the syntactic poise of standard Hindi and, at moments, by the contemplative gravity of Sanskritic resonance. This layered diction allows Ashodhiya to move effortlessly between intimacy and abstraction, between the spoken and the meditative, without losing authenticity in either register.

The poems gathered here traverse multiple thematic domains, yet they are united by an underlying coherence of vision. Love appears not as romantic excess, but as emotional responsibility; devotion unfolds not through ritual certainty, but through reflective humility; social awareness speaks not in slogans, but in measured moral urgency; and self-realization emerges not as proclamation, but as quiet recognition. Across these terrains, the poet remains attentive to proportion—emotion never overwhelms thought, and thought never extinguishes feeling.

Significantly, Ashodhiya's poetry resists finality. His verses do not rush toward closure or moral declaration. Instead, they cultivate pauses—moments where ambiguity is allowed to breathe, where silence carries as much weight as speech. This quality lends **Antaryātrā** its contemplative texture: the poems invite the reader not merely to read, but to linger, to reflect, and at times, to remain unresolved.

In an age increasingly marked by rhetorical excess and ideological rigidity, such poetic restraint acquires particular value. Ashodhiya does not position himself as a spokesman for doctrines or movements; rather, he writes as a participant in the shared moral life of society. His poetry arises from engagement, not assertion—from observation, not proclamation. This gives his work an ethical credibility that is earned rather than claimed.

Antaryātrā may thus be read as the inward chronicle of a poet who understands that the most enduring journeys are not geographical but moral and spiritual. It is a book shaped by patience, sincerity, and attentiveness—qualities that allow poetry to remain humane even when it confronts pain, injustice, or doubt.

Readers who enter this collection with openness will discover not a single voice, but a sustained conversation—between tradition and contemporaneity, emotion and reflection, self and society. In that sense, **Antaryātrā** does not merely present poems; it offers a mode of seeing. And in doing so, it affirms poetry's continuing relevance as a quiet, enduring force within human culture.

Dr. Babu Ram (D.Litt.)
Head & Chairperson
Department of Hindi
Baba Mastnath University, Rohtak

Critical Introduction

Antaryatrā — The Inner Journey

Poetry, when approached as a mode of inquiry rather than ornament, becomes a discipline of inward attention. It does not merely describe emotion or event; it interrogates experience, examining the subtle relations between self, society, memory, and moral choice. **Antaryatrā — The Inner Journey**, a bilingual and transliterated collection of poems by **Anand Kumar Ashodhiya**, belongs decisively to this reflective mode of poetry. The volume positions the lyric not as confession or spectacle, but as a site of ethical listening—where the interior life of the poet intersects with collective realities.

The organizing principle of the book is suggested by its title. *Antaryatrā* signifies movement within—an inward traversal that unfolds through consciousness rather than geography. This inwardness, however, is not escapist. Ashodhiya's poems repeatedly demonstrate that the inner world is shaped by history, social structures, familial bonds, faith traditions, and moral conflict. The journey inward therefore becomes inseparable from the pressures of the outer world; introspection here is a means of clarity, not withdrawal.

Poetic Orientation and Method

Ashodhiya's poetry is characterized by deliberation and tonal restraint. His poems rarely pursue rhetorical excess or dramatic closure. Instead, they tend toward moments of pause—where thought slows, language thins, and meaning emerges through suggestion rather than declaration. This method aligns him with a tradition of Indian reflective poetry in which inwardness functions as a critical lens.

The poet's voice is best understood as that of an *engaged contemplative*: one who inhabits everyday life—its domestic routines, civic anxieties, devotional practices, and emotional attachments—while subjecting these experiences to sustained moral reflection. The poems often begin in the familiar and proceed toward questioning, allowing ordinary situations to unfold into ethical or philosophical insight.

Thematic Constellations

Rather than presenting a single dominant theme, *Antaryatrā* operates through a constellation of concerns that recur across sections of the book:

- **Interior Ethics:** Many poems explore the tension between outward roles and inward truth—between what is performed and what is felt, between inherited duty and personal conscience.
- **Collective Memory:** National history, sacrifice, and social responsibility surface not as grand narratives but as absorbed experiences, filtered through individual awareness.
- **Faith and Fatigue:** Devotional motifs appear alongside doubt, exhaustion, and silence, reflecting a modern spiritual

condition in which belief must continually renegotiate meaning.

- **Human Vulnerability:** Love, loss, familial bonds, and social injustice are approached without sentimentality, emphasizing dignity, endurance, and moral accountability.

These thematic strands do not resolve into conclusions. Instead, they remain in dynamic relation, mirroring the unsettled nature of contemporary inner life.

Language, Form, and Transliteration

Ashodhiya's original Hindi poems draw upon spoken idiom, regional inflection, and cultural metaphor while maintaining formal discipline. The language favours clarity over ornament, allowing rhythm, repetition, and silence to carry expressive weight. The English transliterations and translations included in this volume are not secondary supplements but integral to the project's design. They extend the poems' reach while preserving their tonal and ethical character.

The act of transliteration here is both literary and cultural: it enables the poems to travel across linguistic boundaries without dissolving their Indic interiority. Certain concepts, rhythms, and silences are intentionally retained, acknowledging that not all meaning is transferable without residue.

Structure and Reader Engagement

The arrangement of poems in *Antaryatrā* reflects a gradual inward movement. Rather than a chronological or thematic rigidity, the structure allows for emotional progression—inviting readers to linger, revisit, and reflect. The book resists linear consumption; it encourages a mode of reading attentive to nuance, recurrence, and pause.

In this respect, the collection challenges contemporary habits of speed and immediacy. It asserts inwardness as a necessary literary and ethical practice—one that demands patience, receptivity, and moral seriousness.

Conclusion

Antaryatrā — The Inner Journey stands as a work of sustained introspection in an age often resistant to inward attention. Anand Kumar Ashodhiya's poetry does not seek to persuade or console; it seeks to recognize—to render visible the silent negotiations that shape human conduct and belief. The poems affirm that the most consequential journeys are those undertaken within, where certainty is rare, language is tested, and conscience remains awake.

As a literary project, *Antaryatrā* contributes meaningfully to contemporary Hindi poetry and its English mediation, offering readers a space where reflection becomes an act of quiet resistance and poetry retains its ethical depth.

Dr. Chander Dutt
Lecturer Hindi
GSSS *Gharwal Sonipat*

Dedication

DEDICATION

To my revered Gurudev,
Śrī Paleram Dahiya Halālpuriyā Ji
Custodian of Ragni, Lok–Geet, and the Living Tradition of Haryanvi Lok–Sanskriti

There are influences that shape a writer not through instruction, but through presence; not through doctrine, but through lived example. My Gurudev, Śrī Paleram Dahiya Halālpuriyā Ji, was such a presence—one whose life itself was a form of teaching.

From the soil of Halalpur emerged a voice that carried far beyond geography. Through Ragni and folk-song, through restraint and dignity, through humour and lament, Gurudev embodied the moral memory of a people. His art was never ornamental; it was ethical. His music did not merely entertain—it preserved, questioned, and transmitted a civilizational rhythm.

What I absorbed from him was not technique alone, but temperament:
the discipline of silence,
the weight of responsibility in utterance,
and the understanding that true expression must arise from inner steadiness rather than outward display.

Antaryātrā — The Inner Journey is born of that inheritance.
If these poems turn inward, it is because I learned

early that depth is reached not by excess, but by listening.
If restraint governs their tone, it is because Gurudev taught—without ever saying so—that art must first answer to conscience.

This book, therefore, is not merely a personal collection of poems.
It is an offering—of gratitude, remembrance, and continuity.
A quiet acknowledgement of a lineage where sound became culture,
and culture became character.

At your lotus feet, Gurudev,
I place this inward journey—
with humility, with reverence,
and with enduring gratitude.

— **Anand Kumar Ashodhiya**

Avikavani Publishers, 2026

PATRIOTIC · NATIONAL PRIDE · TRIBUTE POEMS

Here, the individual voice widens into the cadence of the nation.
These poems arise from a reverent listening to collective memory—
where emotion assumes the weight of history
and belonging is shaped by sacrifice and endurance.

The nation appears not merely as territory or symbol,
but as a living moral inheritance:
the land as memory, the flag as ethical call,
freedom as a slow and costly making.

The tone is one of exaltation tempered by humility—
measured ardour rather than proclamation.
Rhythms echo marches and ballads;
imagery draws upon soil, labour, blood, and resolve
quietly absorbed into time.

What follows is poetry as homage—
not to power, but to conscience;
an inward salutation to courage, memory,
and the shared burden of nationhood.

Vijay Diwas — Victory Day

I

In seventy-one's awakening dawn,
The signs of war began to spawn.
Yahya Khan, with ruthless hand,
Arrested Mujib across the land.
The eastern cries of rebel flame,
Were crushed beneath the tyrant's name.
The army's rage spread far and wide,
Innocence suffered, none could hide.
Leave those tales of pain behind —
Let me take the story's next line.

II

Prime Minister Indira's heart was sore,
At Pakistan's deceit once more.
With Manekshaw she sat in thought,
To know what counsel wisdom brought:
"Can we strike by April's end?" she asked,
But monsoon's clouds the General tasked.
He said, "Without due time, I'd fail."
So patience ruled, not war's avail.
Leave those moments where they lie,
Let me tell what happened nigh.

III

On third December, fate did play —
Pakistan lost its mind that day.
Its foolish men, in blind disdain,
Blew horns of war across the plain.
On India's airfields bombs were thrown,
Yet courage in our hearts had grown.
Indira called her council near,
And steered the nation without fear.
Leave that night of sudden cry,
Let me tell what followed by.

IV

By striking first, they sealed their doom —
For India rose to pierce the gloom.
In East, the troops of Chittagong,
Freed every inch where chains had long.
Jessore, Khulna — victory's flame,
And Dhaka next, the final aim.
The MiG-21s took to sky,
Prepared for battle, swift to fly.
Leave those echoes where they lie,
Hear the next — the tale draws nigh.

V

On Dhaka's house of rule that day,
The bombs of India found their way.
The MiGs had torn the rooftop high,
The flag of terror bade goodbye.
Governor Malik's trembling hand,
Signed his end, as truth did stand.

Resigned beneath the flaming sky —
Leave that scene, now pass it by.

VI

Niazi's heart could bear no more,
Defeat knocked loud at every door.
On Sixteenth December — glory's sign!
He laid his arms, his men, his line.
Ninety-three thousand soldiers bound,
As prisoners on Indian ground.
East was free — the dawn was bright,
Bangladesh born from freedom's light.
Leave those triumphs in the sky,
Let me tell the reason why.

VII

Four thousand brave, with blood divine,
For Mother India chose to shine.
Their names we chant on Victory Day,
Whose valor paved the nation's way.
Come, bow our heads to heroes' grace,
Whose souls still guard this sacred place.
And if the call of war we hear —
We'll kiss our swords without fear.
Yes, if the call of war we hear —
We'll kiss our swords without fear.

MATRUBHUMI — "Motherland"

When martyrs fall — their blood a sacred wreath,
They come back crowned beyond the bravest's breath.
Even heroes' hearts in hush and terror meet,
At sight of those who lay their lives at feet.
My mother bore a lion — I'll not disgrace her name;
I'll march with drums to battle, burn the foe with flame.
Not everyone is fated for such glorious end —
To sleep within the soil where once their childhoods spend.
I'll kiss this earth, and mark my brow with sacred sign,
Then roar my challenge, beat the war-horn's brassy line.

Whenever the land shall call, I stand — at India's side,
There is no life above my country's guarded pride.
For motherland I'll never flinch, nor ever step aside,
Adorned with valor in the fray — the world shall see my stride.
Clad in the tricolour when last I wrap my frame, no tear I'll shed,
Let not my sacrifice be vain — shout Bharat's slogan spread.
In blood's fierce Holi I will bathe the foe and make them rue,
Then guard my mother's soil and slip to sleep in peace anew.

Independence Day

Upon the altar of Freedom's flame, how many lives were given,
Countless souls toiled for the land — till liberty was risen.
For those who perished, lost to fame, today their names I call,
The unsung martyrs of our soil — I bow to one and all.

Chandrashekhar Azad, Bhagat Singh — their names resound in light,
Lal, Bal, Pal and Gandhi ji — forever in hearts ignite.
Lala Lajpat bore the blows, for freedom's noble fight,
Countless souls toiled for the land — till dawn replaced the night.

Forgotten heroes, I recall — their glory I renew,
Their memory flames within my verse — eternal, pure, and true.
When passion for freedom filled each heart, the nation's song was made,
Countless souls toiled for the land — and freedom's debt was paid.

Aurobindo and Barindra Ghosh, brave Bhupendra Nath too,
Shiv Verma, Batukeshwar Dutt, and Khudiram — heroes true.
When revolution's trumpet roared, the tyrant's pride did fade,
Countless souls toiled for the land — their courage never swayed.

Uyyalawada Narasimha Reddy — Andhra's valiant name,
Jatin Mukherjee and Prafulla Chaki — lit the rebel flame.
"Quit India!" rose the cry — that shook the empire's might,
Countless souls toiled for the land — till dawn replaced the night.

B. C. Vohra, Rajendra Lahiri, Ram Prasad Bismil strong,
Rajguru, Sukhdev, Roshan, Ashfaq Ullah — sang that song.
From Kakori to the Assembly's fire, their fame did brightly blaze,
Countless souls toiled for the land — through deathless, fearless days.

Vinayak Damodar Savarkar — the lion unafraid,
Veer Bhai Kotwal, Bipin Chandra Pal — by courage made.
Vanchinathan's fiery stand — drove British might away,
Countless souls toiled for the land — that freedom's sun may stay.

Madan Lal Dhingra, P. M. Bapat, S. K. Verma gave their breath,
Lala Hardayal, Sachin Sanyal, Surya Sen embraced their death.
When Surya Sen stormed Chittagong, his name in gold arrayed,
Countless souls toiled for the land — till liberty was made.

Basanta Biswas, Chatterjee, Rash Behari Bose arose,
Barin Ghosh and Jugantar flames — Bengal's

proud throes.
Delhi's bomb had thundered loud, the Viceroy's fear displayed,
Countless souls toiled for the land — till dawn replaced the shade.

Pritilata, Beena Das, and Rani Lakshmi Bai — the brave,
Durga Bhabhi, Sushila Trehan, Velu Nachiyar — the wave.
These women warriors of the fight — their courage brightly blazed,
Countless souls toiled for the land — and freedom's fire was raised.

Aleemuddin Ahmad, Aruna Asaf Ali — bold and kind,
A. Q. Ansari, Subhash Bose, and Mohan Singh aligned.
Lakshmi Sahgal marched with pride — with INA they swayed,
Countless souls toiled for the land — till liberty was made.

Inayatullah Khan, Nazrul Islam, Mahmud Hasan the wise,
Hemchandra Kanungo, Phadke, Ubaidullah's rise.
Through Quit India's clarion call — the world in awe they laid,
Countless souls toiled for the land — till liberty was made.

Udham Singh's valor — can any heart forget his flame?
Sarojini Naidu, Sardar Patel — immortal in their name.
Ambedkar too, in the nation's cause, his steady hand had played,
Countless souls toiled for the land — till liberty was made.

Har Ghar Tiranga — The Tricolour at Every Home

Let every home hoist the tricolour high,
Let it wave beneath the Indian sky.
O flag of pride, O sacred hue,
May every rooftop honour you.

But—
If you trade in knowledge for gold,
And sell young minds, and hearts are sold;
If education's your market plan—
Then do not raise the flag, O man!

If in khaki you guard the wrong,
And aid the tyrant, the cruel, the strong;
If you bribe the poor to fill your chest—
Then keep your hands from that flag's crest.

If, posing as God on earth you stand,
And cheat the people across the land,
O hypocrite saint, false in fame—
Do not raise the tricolour's name.

If healers dressed in white deceive,
And from the sick their dues retrieve,
O doctor who betrays your art—
That flag is not for your blackened heart.

If sworn by Gita you still lie,
And twist the truth for gain and tie;
O lawyer cloaked in dark deceit—
That flag is not for hands unclean.

If merchants mix with poison trade,
And hoard the goods the poor have made,
If greed has darkened all your soul—
The flag shall not adorn your role.

If public trust you claim to own,
But break each promise once you've grown;
O selfish leader, cunning dove—
Do not raise the flag of love.

If you've sworn by the Constitution's might,
Yet sold your post for coins at night,
If justice sleeps beneath your reign—
Then hoist no flag, for it's in vain.

If you kill the girl before her birth,
And mock her tears, her dreams, her worth;
O cruel heart, by greed defiled—
You've no right to honour that flag's child.

If labour's sweat you steal away,
And hoard the wealth they earn each day,
If you rob the nation's open door—
Then wave that flag of ours no more.

Kargil Vijay Diwas — The Ballad of Kargil Glory

The Himalaya stood in silent grief, its peaks in frost confined,
It felt the plots of Pakistan, in shadows dark designed.
Amid the snows they crept across, five thousand crossed the line,
They seized the Tiger Hill's high crown — their treachery's sign.

They pitched their tents on stolen heights, hid weapons deep in snow,
Their guns and shells and mortar fire began their deadly show.
But when the news reached India's heart, each soldier's soul caught flame,
Our army moved with lightning speed — to cleanse the land of shame.

Cannons roared, and rifles blazed — the valley shook with sound,
The mountains echoed thunder's call, where courage could be found.
Smoke and fire clouded all, no sun nor path was clear,
The winds themselves were sharp with steel, the air was filled with fear.

In Dras and Mushkoh's icy gorge, the war clouds gathered black,
The foe lay high on stolen peaks, and rained their ruthless attack.
Our troops were trapped below the cliffs, while

death came from above,
Yet still they climbed through biting winds, with faith and fire of love.

Three hundred guns we brought to bear, five thousand shells were cast,
And thunder ruled the mountain sky, as moments fled so fast.
The enemy's pride began to fade beneath our roaring might,
Then from the skies the Air Force came, to join the holy fight.

Without one step across the line, our fighters soared in flame,
They dove through clouds of bursting fire — their courage had no name.
The bombs they dropped in measured wrath, the hills began to quake,
The foes lay shattered, torn and crushed, their dreams began to break.

Seven hundred fell in death, the rest fled down in fright,
The tricolour rose on Tiger Hill — the dawn regained her light.
Five hundred sons of Bharat gave their lives in that fierce fray,
To keep the mother's honour pure, they offered all that day.

And thus the line restored again, our soil was made our own,
The peaks that bled were freed once more, our valor brightly shone.
Seventeen days of raging war — then victory's sun was born,

On July twenty-sixth, we hailed the flag that glory had adorned.

So bow, O land, before their flame — the soldiers brave and true,
Who climbed through death for India's name, and painted dawn anew.
For Kargil's heights remember still — each martyr's blood-red ray,
That lights our flag eternally — each *Vijay Diwas* day.

Shaheed-e-Azam Sardar Udham Singh

In Sunam town, in Pilbad's soil, a noble home was found,
A Hindu Kamboj family there, where grace and courage bound.
From mother Narayan Kaur's womb, a son divine was born—
December's chill in ninety-nine, yet lit a fiery dawn.

The elder, Sadhu Singh by name, the younger, bold and keen,
His father toiled with weary hands, to keep the hearth serene.
When named at last, the younger cub was christened Udham Singh,
For even in his childhood days, he bore a lion's sting.

Orphaned soon, his parents gone, his brother left midway,
In orphan halls he grew alone, with grief as friend and stay.
He joined the British army ranks, in Basra's distant sand,
But left within a single year, to serve his motherland.

Then came the Jallianwala night, that cursed and bloody ground,
Where bullets rained on innocents, and silence had no sound.
His heart caught fire, his soul awoke, beside the

martyr's flame,
He joined with Bhagat Singh in oath—to cleanse the tyrant's shame.

Through Ghadar ranks he rose in might, a rebel forged in pain,
With arms unlicensed, courage bare—arrested once again.
Five years in chains, yet still he burned, his cause a sacred call,
To London's streets his fate would lead, to end the sin of all.

For twenty-one long restless years, that vengeance in him grew,
When would he strike, when would he rise, his every dream he knew.
Then came the thirteenth day of March, in nineteen forty's hour,
At Caxton Hall, his bullets spoke—Dyer's breath had lost its power.

He gave himself in proud arrest, with fearless heart and tone,
"For Mother India I shall die, the cause is all my own."
V.K. Krishna Menon pled his case, yet justice turned to steel,
The British court decreed his fate—a noose, his final seal.

On thirty-first of July that year, he smiled, embraced the sky,
He offered all for Bharat Maa, and dared the world to try.
Across the seas his name resounds, "Ram Mohammad Singh Azad,"

A man beyond all faith or caste—his soul to God, his vow to God.

For thirty-four long patient years, his ashes stayed afar,
Till home they came to Pilbad's earth, beneath his natal star.
So let us bow to Udham Singh, that blazing heart of flame,
Whose martyr's blood still lights our flag, whose courage none can tame.

The Immortal Tale of India's Param Vir — Nirmaljit Singh Sekhon

Let me tell you, friends, today,
of a son of soil, brave and gay —
of **Nirmaljit Singh Sekhon**, the Jat so bold,
whose tale of courage must be told.

In Punjab's heart, near Ludhiana town,
in a village called *Rurka*, fame was born;
'43 — a July morn,
when sunlight kissed the fields of corn.
To Trilochan Singh, an airman known,
was born a boy — Nirmal, his own.
A father's dream, a son's desire,
to touch the sky, to climb still higher.
And in the year of sixty-seven's June,
his wings took flight beneath the moon.
He joined the Air Force, young and keen,
to guard the land, to serve the Queen.

Hear now the saga, brave and bright —
of Nirmaljit Singh Sekhon's fight.

At Srinagar Base he took his stand,
amidst the snows, the icy land.
Each day he soared on *Gnat*'s steel wings,
to where the cloud and thunder sings.
Duty rose as ranks did rise,
to guard the base was now his prize.
Through mountain winds and blinding snow,
his moustache firm, his eyes aglow.
Each dawn he'd shout his nation's cry,
"Jai Hind!" and take to sky.

Hear now the saga, fierce and bright —
of Nirmaljit Singh Sekhon's fight.

'71 — December morn,
Pakistan's wrath on wings was borne.
On Srinagar base the sirens cried,
six Sabre jets came, death their guide.
The *Flying Bullets* of Squadron Eighteen,
took to the air with engines keen.
Nirmal was ready, swift and sure,
his courage pure, his aim secure.
No delay, no moment lost,
he faced the foe, whate'er the cost.

Through fog and mist that cloaked the ground,
the roar of jets, the deadly sound;
he sighted one, then aimed his gun,
and down it went — his work begun.
Then turned his sights on number two,
a flash of flame — the Sabre flew!
His commander called, "Be cautious, son!"
He only smiled — "This fight's not done!"

Hear now the saga, burning bright —
of Nirmaljit Singh Sekhon's fight.

"I won't let these demons cross our land,
while breath still stirs within my hand.
Two I chase, and more shall fall,
till death itself comes with its call."
Then silence fell across the skies —
his final cry, his last goodbyes.
His Gnat was hit, in flames it spun,
his war was fought, his duty done.

The wreck was found in a distant glen,
but never his body — never again.

Yet the foe fled back, their pride undone —
for one had fought, as fought not one.

**Hear now the saga, pure as light —
of Nirmaljit Singh Sekhon's fight.**

At twenty-eight he met his fate,
but six he faced, and none escaped.
Two downed, four fled — in shame, in fright,
he burned his name in freedom's light.
Posthumous honour — the nation's tear,
Param Vir Chakra, India's cheer.
Statues rise where heroes stand,
songs still echo through the land.
O brave Sekhon, "Anand Shahpur" prays —
may you return in future days.
Each year thy name the people cry,
beneath the tricolour's waving sky.

**Of India's hero, let me tell once more —
Nirmaljit Singh Sekhon, ever adored.**

Netaji Subhas Chandra Bose Jayanti (23rd January)

On the twenty-third, to India Gate, my reverent steps shall go,
Before Netaji's statue there, my floral tributes I'll bestow.
A garland bright with pride and tears, upon his form I'll place,
In honour of that valiant soul — the glory of our race.

His statue now at India Gate, unveiled with nation's grace,
On *Parakram Diwas*, shines forth — a symbol of courage's face.
Without the martyrs' sacrifice, could freedom ever be won?
It was Netaji's dauntless might that made the tyrants run.

His intellect, his blazing will — none ever can forget,
One roar of his could shake the world, and tyrants' power beset.
"Give me blood, and I'll give you freedom!" — his call divine,
That single cry awoke a land — a fire through every spine.

The bravest of the brave he was, with courage fierce and high,
Whose very name still lights our hearts and lifts the nation's sky.
To such a hero bold and pure, my flowers of faith I bring,
Saluting all the martyrs too — *Jai Hind!* forever sing.

Agniveers Shall Choose Their Fiery Path

This call is for service — not a job for pay,
Serve your Motherland freely, with heart's pure ray.
The Army's no trade, no burdened chore —
It's valour's vow, forevermore.

The dull, the soulless, those lost in greed,
Who mock their land in word and deed —
Such selfish minds, devoid of flame,
Would sell their soil for petty fame.

Deluded, bitter, blind they steer,
How could they ever the nation rear?
They're parasites who light the pyre,
Then hide behind their coward's fire.

The cultured, the disciplined youth shall rise,
With new horizons in their eyes.
The rebels burn their nation's name,
While heroes guard her sacred flame.

Those whose veins with patriot's zeal run true,
Are sons of Bharat, brave and new.
They'll march the *Agnipath* with pride,
For Mother India, side by side.

A chance to serve, a golden call,
To give your life — the greatest call.
The world may chase its wealth and gold,
But soldiers' deeds are tales retold.

If you have courage — step through fire,
The Army's path is no desire
For wages, comfort, worldly gain —
It's forged in duty, forged in pain.

This isn't a job — it's a volcano's gate,
Where Agniveers meet their fiery fate.
Let only those with hearts of flame,
Walk Agnipath — in glory's name.

HARYANA — THE STATE SONG

In northern heart of India's land,
there blooms a realm so proud, so grand —
The land of Haryana, green and fair,
of milk and curds beyond compare.
Land of Sindhu's ancient birth,
cradle of Vedic song and earth,
Origin of the Gita's flame —
Haryana bears that holy name.
Pride of fields, of farmer's hand,
leader of the Green Revolution's stand.
The land of milk and curd divine —
O Haryana, glory thine!

From holy Kurukshetra's field,
where truth and dharma once were sealed,
to Panipat's fierce battles three,
Haryana shaped our destiny.
Its soil remembers every fight,
where heroes rose for truth and right.
Pride of fields, of farmer's hand,
leader of the Green Revolution's stand.
The land of milk and curd divine —
O Haryana, glory thine!

Bound south by Delhi, Rajasthan,
and west by Uttar Pradesh's span,
to north lie Punjab, Himachal's crest,
where mountain winds in silence rest.
From Aravalli to Shivalik line,
its ridges rise, its rivers shine.
Pride of fields, of farmer's hand,
leader of the Green Revolution's stand.

The land of milk and curd divine —
O Haryana, glory thine!

Surajkund and Badkhal lake,
the beauty of the land awake;
Hathnikund and Brahma's pool,
make waters sacred, calm, and cool.
Tajewala, Kaushalya's flow,
bring life to every seed we sow.
Pride of fields, of farmer's hand,
leader of the Green Revolution's stand.
The land of milk and curd divine —
O Haryana, glory thine!

Yamuna, Ghaggar, Indira's stream,
sustain the farmer's lifelong dream.
Markanda's banks and Saraswati's trace,
give sacred rhythm to this place.
Through Sutlej link, a history spun —
a tale of progress newly done.
Pride of fields, of farmer's hand,
leader of the Green Revolution's stand.
The land of milk and curd divine —
O Haryana, glory thine!

The farmers strong, the sons of toil,
bring honour to their sacred soil.
Tall young soldiers, brave and free,
the pride of every family tree.
Healthy hearts and sturdy frame,
build people's power, earn their name.
Pride of fields, of farmer's hand,
leader of the Green Revolution's stand.
The land of milk and curd divine —
O Haryana, glory thine!

In global sports, you stand the best,
your champions outshine the rest.

In milk and industry's bright race,
Haryana holds the foremost place.
With skill and labour, youth arise —
self-reliant, bold, and wise.
Pride of fields, of farmer's hand,
leader of the Green Revolution's stand.
The land of milk and curd divine —
O Haryana, glory thine!

The poets, bards, and singers dear,
from Haryana's soil appear.
Their songs in *Raagni's* native tone,
make this land forever known.
Lakshmi Chand — the Sun of Song,
Mangey Ram — whose words belong
to people's hearts, to folk and art,
their music beats in every heart.
Pride of fields, of farmer's hand,
leader of the Green Revolution's stand.
The land of milk and curd divine —
O Haryana, glory thine!

So let us pledge, both hand and heart,
to raise this state in every part.
Shout *Jai Haryana!* loud and clear,
let every soul and voice revere.
Think not of past, but build anew,
a brighter dawn for me and you.
Pride of fields, of farmer's hand,
leader of the Green Revolution's stand.
The land of milk and curd divine —
O Haryana, glory thine!

Through learning's light, through welfare's plan,
we'll lift each child, each woman, man.
Save the daughters, teach them high,
let knowledge spread beneath the sky.
Clean and bright each home and town —

let shining Haryana wear its crown.
Pride of fields, of farmer's hand,
leader of the Green Revolution's stand.
The land of milk and curd divine —
O Haryana, glory thine!

Constitution Day

Heartfelt greetings to the nation, on this
Constitution Day divine,
For through it came true freedom's soul, in
justice's sacred shine.

Though we won our liberty in '47's radiant dawn,
No guiding law yet bound the realm our heroes
stood upon.
Then rose the makers of destiny's plan,
A committee of wisdom — with Ambedkar as the
man.
In two years and eleven months of toil and grace,
Our Constitution took its noble place,
A charter of faith, of freedom's pure array —
That glorified our land in a grander way.

Three hundred ninety-five Articles, eight Schedules
complete,
Twenty-two Parts — a structure strong and neat.
Simple, solid, just, and fair,
Secular, social, democratic in care.
It guards all classes, harms not one,
A lamp of equality under the sun.
When on 26th November '49 it came alive,
The Assembly rejoiced — a proud nation did revive.

Now every year, on this sacred date,
India celebrates, proud and great.
It reminds us all of rights and duties true,
And the law that protects both me and you.
Salute to those who framed this guide,
Our nation's honour, its steadfast pride.
May these principles ever stay —
To guard our people, light their way.

LIFE-PARTNER

(Reflections of an Airman's Wife)

As youth's bright bloom began to rise,
my parents' hearts grew full of sighs.
The snow-haired aunties soon appeared,
with toothless smiles and blessings cheered.
They praised my glow, my "bridal grace,"
and gossiped dreams of a wedding face.
Each whispered plan, each hopeful scheme,
filled mother's ear with marriage dream.
Even neighbours sang that single song —
"When will her wedding come along?"

After much thought and searching wide,
a match was found — my parents' pride:
a handsome airman, brave and tall,
their final choice — the best of all.
My friends burst out in teasing glee,
with tales of army's foolery.

Reena began, "Listen, dear, I'll tell —
of soldiers and their brains as well!
Once a man walked down the street,
the doctor saw him, rose to greet:
'Oh my! You're back after five long years,
your brain's still on my table here!'
The man replied, without a frown —
'Keep it, doc! I've joined the crown —
the Army now — I've no more need,
of brains or thought — just faith and deed!'"

I laughed but sighed — and calmed my heart,
as wedding day drew close to start.
Dreams fluttered soft — the world grew new,
the air was shy, the sky was blue.
At last the date arrived in grace,

a blush spread gently on my face.
My heart beat fast — oh do not ask,
how restless was my bridal mask!

Softly stepping, he entered in,
he coughed, then smiled — and what a grin!
Behind my veil I dared to see —
his face was pure filmy poetry.
He spoke of love, of stars, of skies,
of mountain winds and firefly eyes.
His honeyed words, his playful art,
bewitched my ears and stole my heart.

Five days later, we were bound,
to his Air Force unit's distant ground.
That very night, a neighbour fair,
invited me to dine with care.
By next day's dawn, I'd made my start,
to run my small domestic part.
After much pleading and a quest,
a shared small quarter was our nest.

At morning's horn, he leaves for flight,
returns at ten for toast and bite.
And what to say? My clever man —
made sofas out of tins and cans!
But mind you, don't you think it plain —
he bought a coloured TV again!

In style and trend, he leads the way,
next only to the stars of play.
Once a week we dine in town,
on Hero Honda he takes me round.
Where demons fear and angels hide,
we're posted there — yet live with pride.

That foggy mirror of my past,
now shows its truth — so clear, so vast.

To wed an airman, bold and free,
was the best that fate could give to me.
Those suitors — doctors, lawyers, men —
all seem like rivers that dry again.
While Airmen — they're the fiery streams,
of lava, courage, life, and dreams.

So listen, maidens, to what I say —
choose an airman, if you may.
For lucky are those who serve the land,
and blessed are we, who hold their hand.

National Language — Hindi

Hindi — our national tongue,
India — our sacred song.
Let Hindi rise in every way,
Let this be the nation's say.

Together we pledge, hand in hand,
To honour Hindi across the land.
In thought, in word, in deed we'll stand,
To bring her lost glory back so grand.
The Constitution's spirit — clear and pure —
Makes this our duty, proud and sure.
Hindi — our national tongue,
India — our sacred song.

Let Hindi grow beyond mere speech,
To offices and pens may it reach.
The people's voice, the writer's art,
The nation's pulse, the people's heart.
In every file, in every plan,
Let Hindi serve the common man.
A billion souls in love declare —
Hindi, our mother beyond compare.
Hindi are we, Hindi our flame,
India and Hindi — one in name.
Hindi — our national tongue,
India — our sacred song.

On global stage, let Hindi shine,
With pride, with grace, with voice divine.
In treaties, talks, and grand affairs,
Let Hindi breathe in global airs.
For every son and every daughter,
Let Hindi be their soul and charter.
Let its glory reach the skies,

Till all the world in praise replies.
And echoes through the vast Akasha —
"Hindi — the pride of Hind, our rasa!"
Hindi — our national tongue,
India — our sacred song.

DEVOTIONAL · SPIRITUAL · PHILOSOPHICAL POEMS

Beyond belief lies inquiry; beyond certainty, contemplation.
These poems turn away from the noise of the visible world
and listen instead to the quieter urgencies within.

Here, devotion is not confined to ritual,
nor philosophy to abstraction.
Faith is questioned, meaning weighed,
and silence becomes a form of speech.
Paradox is not contradiction but illumination;
reflection becomes a mode of prayer.

Moving through allegory, refrain, and aphorism,
these verses seek no final answers.
They offer, instead, meditative pauses—
ethical murmurs, metaphysical hesitations,
and inward dialogues shaped by doubt and wonder.

This section marks a descent into the inner terrain
where belief, conscience, and existence
quietly converse.

Sanātana Dharma — The Eternal Way

Sanātana Dharma is eternal—
born of the first dawn of time.
Forbearance, compassion, and mercy
are woven into every vein of its being.

Call it Hindu, call it Vedic—
the meaning remains the same: eternal.
It is the distilled essence of all faiths,
the most ancient among all ways known to humankind.
Formed for the welfare of all beings,
it stands as the highest moral discipline.
Its three sustaining pillars are Man, Woman, and the Divine—
the Supreme Father, the Preserver,
by whom the universe was brought into being.
Forbearance, compassion, and mercy
are woven into every vein of its being.

Through renunciation and penance
it instilled faith among all.
By lighting the lamps of culture,
it illumined every age.
Bearing peace and harmony,
it cast its light in every direction.
Through unbroken truth and righteousness
it imparted order to the world.
Without beginning, without end,
immutable and steadfast it abides.
Forbearance, compassion, and mercy
are woven into every vein of its being.

Declared in the Vedas and the Purāṇas,
it arises from the Supreme Brahman itself.
Devotion and reverent worship
have awakened countless hearts.
Through true faith and loving surrender
the gravest afflictions are dissolved.
Within every living being dwells the Supreme,
entwined with every breath.
When the final thread is severed,
the soul is said to merge into Brahman.
Forbearance, compassion, and mercy
are woven into every vein of its being.

Formed of *Sat* and *Tattva*,
Sanātana is everlasting, infinite, unceasing.
Life and death are declared eternal truths,
unchanging in their certainty.
The soul—unaging, immortal, indestructible—
is but a reflection of the Supreme Light:
neither burned, nor broken, nor destroyed,
nor ever made visible to the eye.
It merges into the Supreme Radiance
by one who has lived in righteousness.
Forbearance, compassion, and mercy
are woven into every vein of its being.

Selfless service, penance, charity, and compassion—
these are life's sacred values and disciplines.
Let spirituality, prayer, renunciation, and duty
bar the entry of corruption and decay.
Why, O embodied and unknowing soul,
has this precious birth been squandered in vain?
Seek the path of liberation,
and turn toward the gate of release.
Forbearance, compassion, and mercy
are woven into every vein of its being.

Dakṣa Prajāpati Jayantī

(A Commemorative Hymn)

From Brahmā's mind was born that son
who laboured for the earth's release;
King Dakṣa Prajāpati he was named,
by whom creation found increase.

Descending once on Himālaya's crest,
he ruled the lands in ordered might;
subduing kings beneath one law,
he bore the crown of sovereign right.
For sages, ascetics, saints alike
he wrought the work of common good;
gods and demons, gandharvas fair,
and kinnar hosts his greatness knew.
He set in motion dharma's way
and cast unrighteousness aside.

To Prasūti, daughter of Manu's line,
his sacred marriage rite was bound;
ten thousand sons were born of him,
as lord of progeny renowned.
Sixty daughters graced his house—
thus Sati's noble sire was he;
to Śiva, lord of sacred calm,
his daughter's hand he gave decree,
by Brahmā's word this bond was sealed,
a blessing laid on fate's design.

Yet when from Brahmā's fivefold head
one crown by Śiva's hand was shorn,
the king's own heart grew torn within,
his pride to wounded wrath was sworn.
He barred that gentle son-in-law
from sacrificial fire and call;
his daughter Sati, burned by grief,

embraced the flame and suffered all.
The sages of the earth then came
to rites of offering and rite.

Bearing Sati upon his shoulder,
Śiva wandered the grieving land;
wherever fell her sacred form,
there rose a Shakti shrine so grand.
Ten thousand sons of Dakṣa's seed
renounced the world and turned away;
A realm like heaven he had shaped
upon this earth of mortal clay.
Life may depart, yet vows remain—
thus lived his truth, austere and plain.

Each year, as once ordained by time,
the thirteenth day of July returns;
the Prajāpatis gather as one,
with reverent hearts and incense burns.
We, children of Dakṣa's ancient line,
lift now his glory into song;
In honour of that primal sire,
our faith stands firm, our tribute strong.
Among the faithful he abides,
counted in memory and prayer.

SAVERA — The Dawn

Rise, arise! The dawn is here —
The sun's bright chariot flames the sphere.
The birds are singing songs of cheer,
The earth in golden robe draws near.

The new-born rays embrace the day,
They weave new life in every way.
Each moment now with joy is crowned,
New hopes in every heart abound.

It's time to turn your dreams to gold,
The world awaits — be brave, be bold!
Each path will shine with light anew,
For morning's call is meant for you.

Awake, advance, and make your mark,
Let courage kindle from the dark.
Your will shall shift the sky's own hue —
For dawn itself awakens through you.

Message of Life

Let us walk the path where truth's pure light shall glow,
Where every step brings faith, and hearts with courage flow.
Where every whispering breeze carries love's refrain,
And every noble deed makes the world humane.

Let us be those rays that drive the dark away,
Lighting hearts with hope, to bring a brighter day.
Let us turn this earth to heaven, with songs of grace,
Where love unites all souls—no walls, no race.

Let us be those clouds that cool the weary land,
And gift each saddened face a smile so grand.
Where in the flight of birds, freedom's music rings,
And children's laughter blooms—like springtime sings.

Let us raise the weapon that spreads the light of truth,
Ignite each corner bright with wisdom's proof.
Let us walk the path of humankind's embrace,
Till evil fades, and virtue takes its place.

This is life's message—let all hearts understand,
To make each day more beautiful, each bond more grand.

Time

Man — the slave of Time,
Man — the sovereign of Time.

He alone perceives the Truth,
He alone upholds the Faith.
He knows of Rama —
Yet, he remains the slave of Time.

He chisels lies into shapes,
And denies what truth creates.
He bows to lust and pride —
Still, he's the slave of Time.

He slays his fellow man,
Yet mends the broken life again.
He bears the name of valor —
And still, the slave of Time.

He is the mirror of his age,
The guardian of a woman's grace —
Yet he stains his very name.
Still, the slave of Time.

He wears the mask of cowardice,
He breathes the form of death,
Yet bears the visage of the Divine —
Man, the slave of Time,
And the lord of Time alike.

LOVE · ROMANTIC · LOSS · LYRICAL POEMS

Here, emotion finds its most human music.
Love enters not as ideal or abstraction,
but as lived presence—
tender, fractured, remembered, and mourned.

These poems return to the intimate terrain of longing:
desire spoken softly, affection shaped by time,
loss carried not as spectacle
but as quiet residue.
Joy appears fragile, fleeting, yet luminous.

Voices speak in half-confession, half-song,
through repetition and refrain,
through the rhythms of closeness and separation.
The language remains personal, sometimes restrained,
sometimes rustic, always honest.

What follows is lyric truth—
the unfinished record of the heart:
vulnerable, incomplete,
and unmistakably human.

I Will Not Wear the Red Sari, O Beloved King

I will not drape the red sari, O my king,
Its colour may stain your soul.
I will not tie the anklets, O my king,
Their touch may pierce you, wound you whole.

I will not veil myself in a chunari,
Lest it displease your tender heart.
I will not leave my hair unbound,
It may shadow your face, hide your light.

I will not darken my eyes with kohl,
Its hue may colour your gaze.
I will not wear the nose-ring bright,
Its edge may prick you, cause you pain.

I will not dye my lips crimson-red,
Its tint may spill upon you so.
I will not chew the betel leaf,
Its colour may upon you flow.

I will not wear the dangling earrings,
They may wound you with their sway.
I will not clasp the golden hansli,
Its touch may sting you, night and day.

I will not don the blouse and choli,
If they fail to please your mind.
I will not bind the waist with bands,
If your heart feels left behind.

I will not tie the girdle tight,
It may bruise you unaware.

I will not wear the tinkling bells,
They clatter loud, disturb the air.

I will not wear the anklets fine,
They may pierce you with their sound.
I will not fasten noisy charms,
That raise vain echoes all around.

I will not drape the red sari, O my king,
Its colour may stain your soul.
I will not tie the anklets, O my king,
Their touch may wound you, take their toll.

The Soaked, Subtle Veil

(Verse 1)
What's it to you, what's it to you,
If I die a thousand ways?
Ah, what's it to you, my love,
If I fade in the misty haze?

(Chorus)
I rain like a darkened cloud tonight,
I soak like a veil so fine and white,
A drizzle of pain, a storm of sighs,
Falls softly through my weary eyes.
Still—what's it to you, what's it to you,
If I die a thousand ways?
Ah, what's it to you?

(Verse 2)
You never came, nor sent a word,
My waiting eyes—forever stirred.
They gaze the road, they ache, they plead,
For a trace of love, a tender deed.

(Bridge)
You took too long, too long to see,
This rain was born of misery.
Each drop a wound, each sigh a scar,
Still—you stand where shadows are...

(Final Chorus)
I rain like a darkened cloud tonight,
I soak like a veil so soft, so slight,
A drizzle of grief, a whispered call,
That drenches my soul, once and for all.
And still—what's it to you, my love,
If I die a thousand ways?
Ah, what's it to you?
Ah... what's it to you...

When Your Memory Came Again

You left me, turned your face away —
And took along those golden days.
I trembled within, dying each breath,
When your memory came again.

The bundle of your memories —
You'd tied and hid somewhere deep.
I wished to stop my breath — but no,
You dwelt in every breath I keep.
My soul got trapped, entangled fast —
When your memory came again.

My heart once smiled — a little peace returned,
But soon the calm was gone again.
The streams went dry, my eyes too burned,
As they waited long in vain.
My weary eyes still search your path —
Faded now, your memory remains.

You turned to void, and I to numb,
My being lost all trace.
Destroyed to the root, crushed in pain —
Paid the debt with tears and grace.
You took both breath and soul away —
Then returned — your memory again.

I gave my life, my wisdom too,
Still you haunt, won't set me free.
In the supreme light I merged at last —
Yet you linger, shadowing me.
My soul still roams, forever asks —
Why must your memory come to me?

THE REAL PAIN

You left me, girl — I didn't grieve,
You stopped speaking — I still could breathe.
But the real pain struck me through —
When you saw me once... and ignored me too.

I cried my nights, I burned my days,
Lost my peace in a hundred ways.
But the real pain broke me through —
When on the phone... you blocked me too.

I fought my heart, I tamed desire,
Tried to quench love's mad fire.
But the real pain — it pierced me through,
When you boasted off of your friends... in front of me too.

My heart rebelled, then fell apart,
Love's vessel cracked — and lost its art.
But the real pain — the deepest hue,
Was when for strangers' money... you twisted through.

In strangers' arms you found your rest,
And forgot the love I once confessed.
But the real pain, sharper than before,
Was when you wrapped a snake —adorned,
Like jewels you wore — so cold, so scorned.
O cunning heart, your poison burned,
You killed the peacock — love I'd earned.

O My Beloved, I Will Not Deny You

Dive, my love, into the river of passion —
O my beloved, I will not deny you.
Without you, this life feels barren,
Lonely, aching — it cannot move on, it cannot move on.

The chamber of my heart lies silent,
No one else will ever claim it.
Come, touch the edge of my love,
Let no other hand profane it.
Our days of life are few, my dear,
Each breath is fleeting, each night short-lived —
O my beloved, I will not deny you.

My youth is bound to your name,
My lips — the cup of your desire.
Come, drink this goblet of love,
I will hold nothing back, my fire.
I am yours; you are mine,
Each breath repeats this vow divine —
O my beloved, I will not deny you.

Do not awaken my restraint,
Do not test my trembling passion —
For if you draw me close, my love,
All reason will abandon compassion.
Our eyes have crossed their spellbound line,
And now, by God, we cannot unwind —
O my beloved, I will not deny you.

Payaliya (The Anklet Song)

Part I

Girl:

Your cheap little anklets, my love,
Go *run-jhun, run-jhun* as you walk—
I fear the world might hear their tune,
And learn the love my heart won't talk.

Boy:

Your tiny dusky heart, my dear,
Goes *dhak-dhak, dhak-dhak* all the time—
Whether you know it or I do,
It trembles without reason or rhyme.

Girl:

When I pass through streets and lanes,
Your anklet turns into my foe—
Cham-cham, chhan-chhan, chhamm-chhanan,
It rings and won't let silence grow.
At times it soothes, at times it taunts,
At times it pricks, oh sly and wild—
Why do you tease me so, my love?
I cannot read your tricks, my child.

Girl (refrain):

Your cheap little anklets, my love,
Go *run-jhun, run-jhun* as you walk—
I fear the world might hear their tune,
And learn the love my heart won't talk.

Boy:

Don't cast those eyes so full of fire,
Don't dress and preen with such desire,
Don't toss your curls and set them right,
You strike my soul with lightning bright.
Each day you visit all my dreams,

And flaunt your smile like moonlit streams—
Oh sweetheart mine, have mercy too,
Don't charm me so the way you do.

Girl (final refrain):
Your cheap little anklets, my love,
Go *run-jhun, run-jhun* as you walk—
I fear the world might hear their tune,
And learn the love my heart won't talk.

Boy (echo):
Your tiny dusky heart, my dear,
Goes *dhak-dhak, dhak-dhak* all the time—
Whether you know it or I do,
It trembles without reason or rhyme.

Reply to My Letters, Beloved

I beg of you, my love — reply to my letters, do.
If not to me, then at least — let my letters reach you too.
It feels like ages since your words last came,
And in their silence, I burn in your name.

Perhaps you don't even realize this ache,
Or maybe replies aren't the custom you make.
But one day, my darling — you'll write, won't you?
If not today, then when skies turn blue.

Day by day, I pass this way,
Everything's hollow since you're away.
Nights won't end, your memory stays,
Your face won't leave my heart's gateways.

Sweet weather brings your sweet recall,
Our vows, our promises — they haunt it all.
If only you were by my side,
I'd stop these tears I cannot hide.

For you, I left the world behind,
The spark of your love set fire to my mind.
Your memory's portrait fans that flame —
Keeping alive your whispered name.

What more to write, my dearest soul?
This pain of parting takes its toll.
Your absence weighs — I can't go on,
This lonely dusk feels far too long.

For you are my sweetest dream come true,
My open book of love — all through.
You are the wine that overflows the cup,
The rose just bloomed — the world lit up.

You are the fire of *Heer* and *Laila's* lore,
The sum of love — and yet still more.
Oh beloved, you are — what all hearts adore.

The Thread

Beloved, O soul of my soul,
Don't go far, don't ever go far from me.

When you drift away, my heart begins to weep,
When you are near, my joy runs deep.
And when my heart rejoices, it hums this refrain —
Don't go far, don't ever go far from me.

All joys of the world bloom only with you,
My colours, my life, are tinted by you.
You are the kite of love that soars in my sky —
Don't shake the thread, don't let it fly.
Don't go far, don't ever go far from me.

Beloved, O soul of my soul,
Don't go far, don't ever go far from me.

NAZAR (The Look of Love)

Don't turn away your gaze, don't hide your sight,
Let no one cast an evil eye tonight —
On my crazy beloved, my heart's delight.
Shoot your arrows of glance with might,
Lock your eyes, let them ignite,
But turn away from my lover's sight —
Turn away from my lover's sight.
Shoot your arrows of glance with might.

Don't turn away your gaze, don't hide your sight,
Let no one cast an evil eye tonight —
On my crazy beloved, my heart's delight.
Shoot your arrows of glance with might.

With eyes, scatter seasons bright,
With eyes, conceal the love's invite;
With eyes, bewitch and softly tease —
But spare my darling's eyes, please!
Spare my darling's eyes, please!
Shoot your arrows of glance with might.

Don't turn away your gaze, don't hide your sight,
Let no one cast an evil eye tonight —
On my crazy beloved, my heart's delight.
Shoot your arrows of glance with might.

My Heart of Glass

My heart of glass — you shattered it cold,
Broke it apart, left sorrow to hold.
You broke my heart, my cruel beloved,
And bound my soul to grief instead.

Your tender memories haunt my days,
Your tresses, dark foes, block my ways.
Even the breeze, once kind and near,
Has turned away, estranged and clear.
You broke my heart, my cruel beloved,
And bound my soul to grief instead.

In love's deep sea, a storm arose,
My eyes grew clouds, where sorrow flows.
Then came a rain of tears untold,
And left my eyes with threads of cold.
You broke my heart, my cruel beloved,
And bound my soul to grief instead.

My heart of glass — you shattered it cold,
Broke it apart, left sorrow to hold.
You broke my heart, my cruel beloved,
And bound my soul to grief instead.

I Will Raise a Ruckus

Girl:
Listen, charmer — liar, I see through all your guile;
Don't try to lure me, don't come near — I'll not walk that mile.
Boy:
No, I—
Girl:
Then I'll make noise, I'll make a scene — I'll shout and I'll rile!

Girl:
I know your stories, your songs of false delight,
Don't weave your nets around me — I'll not be trapped tonight.
Boy:
What did you say?
Girl:
I'll call the cops — I'll raise a racket, start a fight!

Girl:
I won't bow down to your show — your carriage or your band,
Your vows are but a glamour — I won't step into your hand.
Boy:
I'm here for you.
Girl:
I'll see you jailed — I'll make a storm — I'll sound the land!

Girl:
Your promises are empty, your dreams a hollow art,
Lies sit on every pledge you shape — you play a

crooked part.
Boy:
Shall I fool you then?
Girl:
I'll turn the tables — raise the din — expose your heart!

Girl:
Just tell me truth — be honest now, reveal what's in your chest;
Why dodge and scheme? If I'm your one, then prove you're truly blessed.
Boy:
I will come —
Girl:
Don't reach for me — I'll make noise — I'll make a test.

Gustakhi Maaf (Pardon My Boldness)

I wipe my eyes and gaze again,
Yet this crowded city pleases me not —
There's only *you* and *I*, my love,
All else fades into naught.

Yes, my beloved, you're not with me,
And life too has lost its spring;
Still, deep within this quiet ache,
Your thought alone does sing.

Hide these feelings, guard your heart,
Let no whisper give them away;
For tongues betray what eyes conceal —
Press your lips, let silence stay.

Memories and longings never die,
They are songs one cannot sing;
They hum beneath the breath of time,
Like an unseen trembling string.

The charms of beauty — I heed them not,
Nor fancy any passing grace;
Your words of love alone I crave,
Your presence fills my space.

Go, someone tell her —

If her curls should touch her cheek,
May I, with pardon, play awhile — *Gustakhi Maaf!*
If her golden form should call to me,
May I, with pardon, hold her a while — *Gustakhi Maaf!*

For every thought that stirs within,
Returns to her, again, again —
How shall I tell her what I feel,
When worry gnaws my heart and brain?

The Letter from My Beloved

1.

O dearest letter from my love,
dearer than my love himself you are —
Born of his affection's flame,
you've become the soul of who we are.

I kiss you soft, I hold you near,
press you close to my beating heart,
My life, my breath — when shall I see
the one from whom you came apart?
For his sweet love alone you came —
you are the reason, you are my star.

2.

I'll lay you under my pillow tonight,
wrap you in dreams so warm and bright,
I'll sing you a lullaby so sweet,
till sleep descends in gentle light.

When dawn awakes, I'll hide you close,
within my breast, safe from the world afar,
Lest any jealous eyes should burn —
you are my life, my guiding star.
For his sweet love alone you came —
you are the reason, you are my star.

3.

Why trembles today my left eye so?
Why comes this hiccup, teasing slow?
Ah! may the wind from eastern skies
bring tidings of the one I know.

My heart takes flight, my spirit yearns,
to reach my love, wherever you are —

O letter mine, you are his breath,
you are my life, my morning star.
For his sweet love alone you came —
you are the reason, you are my star.

May God Forbid

May God forbid — that any lover be torn apart,
May all who love be granted the wish of their heart.
But love so deep is seldom won —
For lovers are gods, and gods are none.

Since I parted ways from you, no shelter have I found,
No corner of the world felt kind, no roof, no sacred ground.
Homeless, hopeless, I wander still,
My only friend — that silent hill.

Yes, I meet that rock each day,
Whisper to it what hearts can't say.
It listens to my weary cries,
And keeps my secret under skies.

I speak to it from morn till night,
Confess my pain in soft twilight.
People see and mock my plight —
They say, "He loves that stone outright!"

But trust me, love — the truth's divine:
The stone I touch, the soul is thine.
Let people gossip all they may,
They sigh in envy, every day.

The stone's but stone, cold and bare —
Yet love for you is written there.
It's only a seat where I sit alone,
To lose myself in your memory's tone.

And when you come, I'll take you there —
To that same stone, to that same air.
I'll show the place where seasons passed,
Where I kept your memory vast.

Though Not You — Your Letter Came

To the drowning heart, a straw appeared —
Though not you, your letter came, endeared.

With trembling hands I broke its seal,
With quivering lips — your touch I feel.
I read it slow, in stammered tone,
And suddenly my soul was not alone.

Your pain I felt in every line,
It pulsed within this heart of mine.
Recalling moments of our embrace,
My heart leapt wild, began its race.

Oh love, don't sink in sorrow's sea,
The hour of union is soon to be.
It feels as though you're here again —
Before my eyes, in flesh, in vein.

Lines of joy shall crown your face,
Fate will soon our love embrace.
Come then, my heart, let's test our stars —
And see how kind our fortunes are.

Beloved (Jaanam)

Beloved... my life, my soul, my own,
Let every age be spent in your arms alone.
Beloved... my life, my soul, my own,
Let every age be spent in your arms alone.

You are the song my lips repeat,
The rhythm my restless heart keeps beat;
This love's a triumph sweet –
Though the world may call it defeat.
O love of mine, what's there to hide?
Let hearts in each other confide.
Beloved... my life, my soul, my own,
Let every age be spent in your arms alone.

You are the light my eyes adore,
The ecstasy my heart implores.
Something untold lies at your door –
Perhaps it's pride in love's pure core.
If that's what keeps you far, my dear,
Tell me softly, let me hear.
Beloved... my life, my soul, my own,
Let every age be spent in your arms alone.

I'm proud, my love, of you alone,
You wear my heart's eternal throne.
Some secret reason makes me shy,
My blushes whisper, yet deny.
Come, let's blend our hearts in tune,
Sing love beneath the silver moon.
Beloved... my life, my soul, my own,
Let every age be spent in your arms alone.

SOCIAL REFORM · PROTEST · HUMAN CONDITION POEMS

Here, the poem becomes witness.
These verses confront the ordinary violences
of inequality, silence, and neglect—
not through abstraction,
but through lived human presence.

When silence becomes complicity,
poetry learns to speak sharply.
Irony tempers anger; realism sharpens empathy.
The personal and the political converge,
revealing society as it is endured, inhabited, and resisted.

Voices shift—from sufferer to observer,
from witness to critic—
employing satire, dramatic irony, folk wit,
and the moral force of realism.

What follows is poetry as conscience:
restless, questioning,
and unafraid to disturb comfort
in the pursuit of dignity.

Female Foeticide

We are the sons of Haryana —
strong as milk, bold as honour's banner.
Our schooling may be poor and plain,
but mansions, cars, and land we gain.

Granaries overflow, the fields are gold,
money heaps high, our pride untold.
We live in style, our feasts are grand,
yet bachelors swarm across the land.

Comforts bloom, but hearts are cold,
our villages echo empty and old.
Boys — the pride of every home,
girls — unwanted, left alone.
Even mothers fear a daughter's birth,
no joy, no song, no sense of worth.

Every man wants a son — an heir,
and sons are born everywhere.
Daughters dry like crops in drought,
Haryana's heart has been turned inside out.

Fewer girls, too many men,
still chasing lineage again and again.
No daughters — no weddings bloom,
no songs of life, just silent gloom.

Our lives are vain, yet pride we keep,
while conscience lies in poisoned sleep.
Each day the unborn daughters die,
and humanity turns a blinded eye.

Men now buy their brides for gold,
for daughters are slain before they unfold.

Sons held high, girls despised,
women forever underprized.

Awake, O people! Now is the time,
erase this ancient, blood-soaked crime.
Give women equal place and pride,
let education be their guide.
Honour the mother, sister, wife,
protect the daughter — cherish life.
End this slaughter of the unborn child,
and see how Haryana smiles — reconciled.
Then every daughter of this land
will proudly rise and make her stand —
"I am Haryana's daughter — alive, unafraid,
unbowed."

Why Should I Become Another Nirbhaya?

Despite the marches, promises, laws we raise,
Each day a new Nirbhaya is lost in blaze.
Enough — trust in humankind has run away,
So tell me now — why should I be one more prey?

Beasts in human skin, with twisted minds that prowl,
Hungry for the hour, for darkness they foul.
Hunters of flesh, blind with lust and greed,
They traffic in torment, in bodies they feed.
If my freedom and my safety I must be my own way,
Then tell me, please — why should I be one more prey?

To wolves who leap toward me, I'll teach them dust and shame,
I'll learn the art of guarding self, and keep my honour's flame.
A daughter to some, a mother, sister, wife to stay —
Then tell me, truly — why should I be one more prey?

Make those ravenous men learn a lesson of our might,
We are not fragile blossoms — we rise in unity and fight.
We're neither prizes for your hands, nor butterflies you sway —
Decide for yourselves, O world — why should I be one more prey?

The Hunger in My Belly Won't Let Me Sleep

The hunger in my belly won't let me sleep,
The shame in my eyes won't let me weep.
The hunger in my belly won't let me sleep.

Whom shall I hide my sorrow from,
And to whom shall I show these wounds that numb?
How do I soothe this gnawing pain,
This hunger that bites again and again?

I wonder why I never earn,
Enough for two full meals in turn;
The meeting of fire and bread is rare —
My empty plate just stares in despair.

Man has eaten man, sold his soul,
While we, the helpless, pay the toll;
Their eyes don't see our starving plight,
Our faces twist in hunger's blight.

Childhood

Homeless, abandoned, cast away —
Wrapped in a tattered cloak of decay,
I stifle sobs that no one hears,
My chest burns low with silent fears.

A hollow stomach — fire-fed,
Trembling limbs, unsteady tread,
I crawl through dust, through hunger's span...
Do you know who I am?
I am the exploited child of this land.

You need not wander far to find me,
No need for pitied search behind me —
Just step beyond your marble gate,
Where refuse heaps await their fate.

There I'll be — scavenging scraps,
Locked in life's relentless traps;
Fighting stray dogs for a bite of bread...
Do you know who I am?
I am the exploited child of this land.

Blind faith, illiteracy, addiction's chain —
These bind my body, numb my brain.
Liquor, opium, smoke and weed,
Are all the gods my sorrows feed.

In some dark alley I may lie,
Silent, soulless, waiting to die;
Or at crossroads, bowl in hand...
Do you know who I am?
I am the exploited child of this land.

Books and learning — strangers all,
No school has ever heard my call.
Manners, morals — words unknown,
In this cruel world, I walk alone.

A mark of shame upon my brow,
"Low-born outcast," they call me now;
Stamped as vile by society's brand...
Do you know who I am?
I am the exploited child of this land.

Cry of the Street-Born Child — To the Doctor

Are you listening, Doctor?
I am crying...
Do you hear me, Doctor?
Do you know why I cry?

My mother—panting, trembling in pain,
Crushed beneath hunger and poverty's chain.
She calls to you, the godlike healer,
Begging for life, her voice growing feebler.
Are you listening, Doctor?
Do you know why I cry?

You—merciless, shameless—crossed every line,
Turned away a dying mother of mine.
Your conduct tore the cloth of honour apart,
Sold your soul, and shamed the healer's art.
Are you listening, Doctor?
Do you know why I cry?

Helpless, she fell upon the street,
Gave birth to me amid dust and heat.
Humanity stood disgraced once more—
India's future was born on the floor.
Are you listening, Doctor?
Do you know why I cry?

If only my mother had understood this nation's disease—
The rot of corruption that kills with such ease,
If only she knew the truth of her land—
Where children are born where pavements stand.
If only she had chosen not to bring me to this strife—

But she gave me, instead, this broken life.
Are you listening, Doctor?
Do you know why I cry?
Are you listening, Doctor?
I am crying...

Autobiography of a Ration-Depot Holder

Four sacks of grain — that's the secret I keep,
My business runs sweet; my profits run deep.
A little dishonesty, a little deceit,
A streak of bad faith — and plunder complete.

If anyone speaks up, there'll be hell to pay,
Sometimes no grain here, sometimes pulses away.
Whoever opens his mouth will lose his share,
I'll sell the half, and half I'll distribute nowhere.

Laws twist and tangle — rules slack at the seam,
From top down to bottom, the whole state's a scheme.
It's not my fault, no— I'm merely a cog,
Born of corruption, grease on the log.

You want to change me? Then change the whole frame:
Rise up, awake, turn politics to shame.
Till that day comes, keep shouting your cry—
Let hunger and malnutrition keep people to die.

Scandal

For days my mind has tossed and turned, a restless, fevered pace,
A demon called—avarice—now claws and crushes all my grace.
The urge to profit by deceit grows strong within my chest,
Where gentleness and decency have slowly been repressed.

My heart conspires: “Commit the fraud, let crooked coin be thine,
Fill up the house with wealth profane — let honesty resign.”
Consume the people’s sweat-won gold, then gulp it down with pride,
Deny each charge with shameless grin, let conscience step aside.

Devour the poor, grow fat and numb, in brazen, shameless sleep,
Cast dust upon the censure’s face and sink in slumber deep.
Those “third-rate” agitators — what terror can they pose?
I’ll snare each mouth that dares to speak, and silence all my foes.

Defeat, disgrace, and punishment — I’ll never change my guise,
With hollow vows and cunning smiles, I’ll crown myself once more to rise.

Let registers of scams be filled — inscribe my name with pride;
And then, like blind Dhritarashtra, I'll close my eyes to every crime.

It Is Necessary That You Fall Silent

It is necessary — that you fall silent,
Lest the veils be torn apart,
Lest some white-robed faces be unmasked —
It is necessary that you fall silent.

Let not your tongue betray the truth,
Let no secret slip its chain —
It is necessary that you fall silent.

Lest black and white get blurred,
Lest virtue lose its name —
It is necessary that you fall silent.

That the "honourable" stay unashamed,
That no saint be stained again —
It is necessary that you fall silent.

For someone's life is now at stake,
And silence is the safer path —
It is necessary that you fall silent.

But if such silence is not possible,
Then sleep — forever sleep —
For even dreams can speak too loud.

Sir, They Call Me Gutkha!

At every corner, every crossroad,
on every Paan stall I stand—
in pouches of every shape and shade,
available to serve your demand.
Yes, I am ever at your command, Sir—
they call me Gutkha!

Come, O come, and bring your friends,
share my joy that never ends;
chew me, taste me, pass me round—
I am cheap, I'm easily found.
Abundant, alluring, always at hand—
they call me Gutkha!

I carry a promise, a dark guarantee—
of throat and cheek and cancer, you see.
In youth itself I bring decay,
I steal your life, sip by day.
Softly, slowly, man by man—
they call me Gutkha!

Cough and phlegm shall join your breath,
your teeth shall rot, your bowels face death;
your kidneys fail, your vigour gone,
the graveyard groans, my victims drawn.
Even the pyres recoil from my clan—
they call me Gutkha!

Not a petty curse, but Death divine,
a god of doom in subtle design.
Yama here, a demon there—
fiercer still than both, beware!
I am the fate of the careless man—
they call me Gutkha!

I'll drain your wealth, your breath, your years,
make you my slave through smoke and tears.
You chew me still, I stand aghast—
your doom is sealed, your end is cast.
And yet you smile, O mortal man—
they call me Gutkha!

Riot – Part I

Overnight, who knows what flared —
The city burned in sudden rage.
From the masses to their chosen men,
Every mask fell off the stage.

Some lost fortune, some lost honour,
Both gambled in the fire's breath;
The tyrants who torched the towns
Now cast their eyes on rural death.

From city to city, village to village,
The agents of death marched wide —
Greedy wolves, drunk on power,
Sat counting coins by corpses' side.

Half-baked bread and burnt dead bodies
Roasted in the same cruel flame —
Thus began a new tradition,
Of hunger and death being the same.

Homeless childhood, ruined youth —
Each ruin bore the city's face;
Those starving for a piece of bread
Sank deeper into poverty's embrace.

I am no coward — I cannot just stand and see;
Nor am I saint enough to bear silently.
My blood boiled at this ghastly sight —
At faith's cruel hands, at humanity's blight.

So I resolved — fierce and fast —
Gathered my wife, my child, my past;
Took what little I owned, fled that land,
Caught the first train — no backward glance.

Politics, deceit, the game of greed,
The barter of gods, the cries of creed —
"Ram, Rahim, Shyam, Ali!" all bled —
Truth and faith — both bought and dead.

Riot — Part II

Peace came back at last — a cautious, fragile truce,
Each face relaxed, believing flames had found their use.
I too returned — a stranger now within my own street,
Measuring every neighbour with suspicion's fleet.

I hailed a rickshaw toward the weary miles,
He drew near smiling, hands raised in greeting's style.
My heart stilled not; I gripped my bundle, cold with fear,
The stranger's smile a mirror that would not clear.

His glance into my eyes stole that small trust away,
And only then my doubting mind could breathe, half-sway.
Through alleys, lanes, I searched each scar the riots made,
Questioned policemen on post as if my calm betrayed.

Till at my stop I fixed my courage, braced my face,
Kept stealing looks in rear-view till the rickshaw paced.
Why did his shining eye awaken deeper dread?
Why did that tiny flash make all my hope feel dead?

"O God," I prayed — "deliver me across this night,
From rickshaw-men who lurk like shadows in my sight."
The rickshaw halted; I trembled, every limb a jar —

He must have felt my fear; his voice cut through the bar:

"Brother, don't you know me? Have you lost your sight?
Remember me? I'm Rehmat — am I still not right?"
Chagrin and startled laughter flushed my bruised disgrace,
And once again I melted into outward life's embrace.

Now like a lion I stride — the riot's storm I scorn,
I fear no mob; I walk my ward as if reborn.
What else can I do — a man — but watch the embers' play?
I bind my things, lay them near, and sleep with one eye sway.

Coalition

Move not an inch without my say,
Be it friend or world — obey my way.
If that cannot be done — then what's this alliance for?
I withdraw my support — for the nation's good, I swore.

Bury the charges made on me,
Let pending cases silent be.
If that cannot be done — then what's this alliance for?
I withdraw my support — for the law's good, evermore.

Give my party's man that chair,
Remove the other — it's only fair.
If that cannot be done — then what's this alliance for?
I withdraw my support — for the ministry's decor.

Announce a package for my land,
Let others suffer — as I command.
If that cannot be done — then what's this alliance for?
I withdraw my support — for my region's good, therefore.

Dark reign, a foolish king — still I backed your throne anew,
Now dance, O ruler, as drums cue you.
If that cannot be done — then what's this alliance for?
I withdraw my support — for the coalition's moral core.

The Loyalty at the Threshold

Everyone knew, yet today I shall tell —
some of my story, some of what befell.
I went to seek a ticket, from a famed party's door,
but the leader began his long, lofty roar.

I said — *"Sir, I'm young, sharp, a leader in the making."*
He said — *"Tickets are for the loyal, not the faking."*
I said — *"I've always stood by the party's side!"*
He said — *"Then show me proof — not just pride!"*

I said — *"I've voted for you, worked all along."*
He said — *"Empty words don't fill the stomach for long."*
I said — *"Here, my record — my loyalty clear!"*
He said — *"A sprain won't heal just by blowing air."*

I said — *"Then tell me, what does loyalty mean?"*
He smiled — *"For thirty-five years I've been sitting at my peer's threshold, unseen."*
I said — *"But I've just stepped into politics, Sir."*
He said — *"Then tell me — whose blessing makes you stir?"*

I said — *"My people, my region stand with me."*
He said — *"Fool! I ask — whose hand is on your head, you see?"*
I said — *"I don't get you, Sir — please speak plain."*
He said — *"Win or lose — no one dares move me from my peer's domain!"*

I said — *"So that's your meaning of loyalty and truth?"*
He said — *"Boy, that's duty — my party's proof."*
I said — *"That's not loyalty — that's being someone's pet."*
He said — *"My peer's like family — your thinking's unfit yet."*

I said — *"I've served the nation; I don't lick boots or tongues."*
He said — *"Then no free ticket for such upright ones!"*
I said — *"The army taught me honesty and grace."*
He said — *"Other contestant lay flowers at peer's feet each day they face."*

I said — *"Forgive me, Sir — I neither crawl nor cheat."*
He said — *"Then, son, no ticket — beggars don't compete."*

"After bowing to the Politician so long,

I dragged my weary soul back home —

face stretched like an old leather boot, faith drained,

yet something raw still flickered within..."

I bowed and went home, silent and sore,
while others made me wear election-glasses, green once more.

And that same leader — the great dispenser of hope —

was trading tickets under the counter's rope.

We stood, ticketless, but upright and clear,
and for that honesty, we earned hatred near.

Many enemies born, only for truth's sake —
I took a vow — *I'll lose, but never fake!*
For when your own kin become traitors inside,
who needs foes — they sit by your side.

So I swallowed the draught of patience and pain,
thinking — *"Brotherhood should somehow remain."*
But they conspired — deceit in disguise,
some perished, some rose — fate's enterprise.

Measured in balance, bound in deceit,
those men were swallowed by time's teeth.
By God's decree, some roots were torn,
some met darkness, never reborn.

And the leader who once gave tickets away,
now stood in line to beg one day.
He got none — his power gone bare,
fate favoured another — justice was fair.

His thirty-five years of "loyalty" went in vain,
his own master cut his chain.
He who once made others crawl,
was left outside — denied by all.

He beat his chest, tore his shirt, cried in pain,
his wealth and deceit — all in vain.
The day his ticket was cut, his voice turned hoarse,
he cursed his fate, his fall, his course.

He quit the party in rage and despair,
betrayed the very cause he used to wear.
He stood with rivals, shameless, loud —
a traitor greater than any in the crowd.

Honour lost, faith decayed,
even loyalty had been betrayed.
He was fooled by the man at whose feet he'd bow —
the same door had kicked him now.

When his own turn came, his loyalty drowned in
oil,
thirty-five years of ties — gone with the spoil.
Those who once sang his loyal song,
now pushed him out — where he belonged.

The book of fate — perhaps by Ram's hand —
wrote justice, firm and grand.
I laugh now, yet inside I reel —
those words, like thorns, I still feel.

A Mother's Wish

O Lord, before Your temple gates, one prayer I repeat –
Grant me a son, befitting the times – my only plea, complete.

I wish not that my son be fair, strong, or hale of frame,
Nor do I ask that he, like Shivaji, win eternal fame.
Let him not be a scholar wise, nor teacher deep and keen,
Nor crowned with glory in assemblies where poets proud have been.

No need that he be gentle, pure, or saintly in his part,
Let not the motherland's defense inflame his loyal heart.
No need for truth to dwell in him, nor honesty to stay,
Let not the righteous path appear before his chosen way.

Then what should he be?

A scheming, lustful, greedy man – a monster in disguise,
Of anger, sloth, and arrogance – with falsehood in his eyes.
A bandit, thug, a robber vile – the devil's very breed,
Let plunder, loot, and violence be the hallmark of his deed.

A turncoat like a rolling stone, a bowl without a base,
A bundle made of hollow lies, with treachery on his face.
Let his stature in politics soar — though his body small remain,
While the common man keeps yearning, yet beholds him all in vain.

For only thus adorned, he'll rise — a *leader* of the land,
Wrapped in cunning's silken cloth, with praises close at hand.

For in this age, all other trades are dying day by day,
But those who enter politics — are clever, wise, and gay.
Before their charm, the seeing turn blind and meek instead,
Their image pure and spotless — while all others painted red.

O Lord, before Your temple gates, one prayer I repeat —
Grant me a son befitting my hope — my only wish complete.

FAMILY · DOMESTIC · PERSONAL SENTIMENT POEMS

Not all journeys are public;
some unfold quietly within shared rooms
and remembered gestures.

These poems dwell in the intimate spaces
of family and kinship—
affection spoken plainly,
emotions shaped by daily life,
love expressed without ceremony.

The language is direct, the rhythm unforced,
the warmth earned rather than declared.
Here, memory becomes shelter,
and the ordinary reveals its enduring grace.

What follows is poetry of closeness—
where tenderness resides in small acts,
and belonging is felt,
not announced.

Father

A mother is shade where tenderness grows,
A father stands firm beneath burning skies.
She binds the world within her gentle veil,
He wrestles roads where every hardship lies.

A mother speaks what the heart longs to say,
A father weaves his love through silent deeds.
No words rest waiting upon his lips—
His affection lives in acts, not speech.

By night and day his sweat becomes the stone
On which the house of hope is firmly laid.
He buries dreams that once were only his,
So children's distant stars may blaze unafraid.

The son moves forward, rising step by step;
Behind him stands a father, smiling low.
Amidst the cheers of crowded celebration,
His joy remains the quietest they know.

Severe he seems—the keeper of all rules,
A sentinel of order, strict and plain.
Yet deep within, a tender ocean flows;
Even his tears he teaches not to name.

A mother nourishes life with flowing grace,
A father gifts the path of self-restraint.
If she is lamp that lights the inner home,
He is the roof that bears each pain.

The mother feels like prayer made visible,
The father—earth itself, profound and sure.
Upon whose back our journeys learn to walk,
Who never seeks a bow, a thanks, or cure.

Only with time we learn to understand
The weight of love that silence had to bear.
A father is not merely word or role—
He is the ground that holds our life in air.

Daughter — A Jewel, a Blessing

A daughter, jewel-like, fortune's grace,
To whom does such a blessing come?
Where a daughter first draws breath,
A father's fate itself is raised.

In her form dwells Lakshmi's light,
She brings her share of destiny.
Her grace, her kindness, quiet strength
Win every heart, the world can see.

Before five years have softly passed,
She learns her mother's ways of care;
At home, she helps with eager hands,
And cradles siblings, laughing fair.
In nurturing her younger ones,
She plays a mother's gentle part.

Like little birds that peck their grain,
She eats but little, gives out more;
She flits through rooms with cheerful sound,
Her presence brightens every door.
Beloved by all the family,
Her tender words make spirits soar.

When grown, she walks the path of books,
Her mind aligned with moral truth;
In learning, play, and discipline,
She often leads beyond the youth.
In work, in skill, in enterprise,
She earns her name, her rightful due.

They call her "wealth that goes away,"
A trust of weight and deep concern;

When wedding fires are lit one day,
New duties wait, new homes to learn.
With tears restrained, her parents give
Their daughter as tradition bids;
The house grows empty, aching still,
When memory of her softly lives.

Leaving parents, kin, and home,
She takes up life's demanding role;
She roots herself in stranger ground,
And builds anew her destined whole.
With patient heart, she bears the ache
Of longing for her childhood days;
From her own womb, new worlds are born—
Creation names her in its praise.

Thus daughters sing a father's worth,
Through lives of love, of care, of light;
A living song of gratitude,
They honour him in quiet might.

The Grandson

The day we heard the joyful word — *"She's expecting!"* —
our home filled up with laughter and light.
Relatives, friends, and neighbours alike,
sang songs of joy from morning till night.

"The firstborn, it must be a boy!" —
each voice declared with gleaming eyes,
and in that echoing hope and joy,
our own hearts too began to rise.

Whenever my daughter-in-law bowed,
to touch our feet with grace and love,
I blessed her gently every time —
"May you bear a son!" from above.

Each month with care, we took her there,
for check-ups, as the doctors told,
ensuring mother and child were well —
her strength and smile turned bright and bold.

With vitamins and milk so sweet,
we fed her every day with glee;
and seeing her glow, her laughter grow,
we said, "A grandson it shall be!"

As months rolled on — three, six, then nine —
we counted days, the hours, the chime;
till came that long-awaited day —
each heart beat fast, in rhythm and rhyme.

At last — the cry! The nurse appeared —
"A girl!" she said with tender cheer.
And suddenly, that golden dream
fell silent in the air, unclear.

Faces turned long, whispers low,
but my wife beamed — a grandma now!
My son rejoiced — a father proud;
and I, the happiest of the crowd!

When I saw my daughter-in-law's eyes,
she smiled and said, half in surprise —
"Father, you'd bless me every day,
'May you bear a son!' — in every way!"

I laughed and said, "I bless again —
O Mother Divine, grant us a grandson!"
The room burst out in laughter loud —
and joy returned to everyone.

The Granddaughter

Poets, singers, writers — all sing of the granddaughter's grace,

But hand on your heart, tell me — do you truly give her a place?

With honeyed words and poetic ink, you praise her on the page,

Yet when she's born, the brightest eyes grow dim with hidden rage.

Your poems ring hollow — gilded lies behind your verse,

For in the craving for a heir, your hearts still rehearse.

We, the fourth pillar, must now hold the mirror high,

Expose the sin of killing girls — before they see the sky.

The nation falls silent — daughters vanish, numbers fade,

The balance of life itself, by man's own hands, betrayed.

Grandsons are adored — apple of every eye,

Granddaughters tolerated — their worth denied.

Everyone wants an heir — the male seed to inherit,

So they seek the doctor's aid, with secret sinful spirit.

If the womb bears a girl — they whisper, "end it, hide it,"

No shame in such a crime — humanity has died in it.

Girls vanish like drought's thirst — look at Haryana's land,

Where grooms now buy their brides, with desperate trembling hands.

Boys abound, girls are few — now see the tragic twist,

Unbalanced lives — tell me, what justice can exist?

Here the murder of unborn girls happens day by day,

While dead humanity lies silent — rotting in decay.

Men buy wives, and sell their souls — the conscience sold, the womb defiled,

They kill the goddess in the cradle — yet call her Mother mild.

Still there's time — awaken, arise, repair!

Give daughters equal love, and rightful share.

Respect your mothers, sisters, wives, and brides —

Protect the girl child — let her live with pride!

Then watch — in every home, joy will bloom again,

And daughters of Haryana shall proudly proclaim —

"I am Haryana's daughter — a granddaughter unashamed!"

The End

Critical Academic And Literary Review

Dr. Pushpa
Professor & Head, Department of Hindi
Maharshi Dayanand University, Rohtak, Haryana

Antaryatrā — The Inner Journey

Poetry, in its most enduring literary manifestations, functions not merely as aesthetic expression but as an epistemic act—an inward probing of consciousness through which unarticulated layers of experience acquire form. **Antaryatrā — The Inner Journey**, a curated bilingual collection of poems by Anand Kumar Ashodhiya, belongs decisively to this tradition of introspective literature, where poetic utterance becomes a mode of ethical and existential inquiry rather than narrative display.

The title **Antaryatrā** (अंतर्यात्रा) is not ornamental but conceptual. It announces the book's central preoccupation with interior movement—a journey enacted within consciousness rather than across spatial or historical coordinates. This inward travel is marked not by resolution but by attentiveness: to silence, fatigue, devotion, doubt, memory, and moral hesitation. Ashodhiya's poems do not seek closure; instead, they cultivate moments of recognition (**anubhūti**), leaving meaning suspended, open, and dialogic.

Poetic Voice and Reflective Temperament

Ashodhiya's poetic voice is characterized by restraint, tonal discipline, and reflective depth. He does not position himself as an ideological polemicist or confessional narrator; rather, he occupies the ethically complex space of a witness—immersed in lived reality yet persistently interrogative of it. The poems often emerge from ordinary sites—domestic interiors, ritual practices, rural memory, historical consciousness—but are transformed through introspection into meditative spaces where personal experience intersects with philosophical reflection.

A notable feature of this poetry is its refusal of rhetorical excess. Emotion is neither dramatized nor sentimentalized; it is absorbed, processed, and rendered with controlled intensity. This restraint lends the poems a quiet authority, allowing moral inquiry to unfold without didactic assertion.

Thematic Architecture: Inward Cartographies

At the thematic core of **Antaryatrā** lies the tension between inner truth and socially inherited roles. Many poems interrogate the exhaustion produced by performative piety, routine morality, and repetitive language. Faith, ritual, and cultural memory are neither rejected nor idealized; they are examined as lived experiences—sometimes sustaining, sometimes depleted, sometimes demanding re-alignment.

Another recurrent motif is existential weariness—not as despair, but as a condition that makes honesty possible. Fatigue here becomes epistemological: it strips experience of illusion and compels a quieter, more durable form of awareness. From this condition arises a poetry that privileges clarity over comfort and truth over consolation.

The collection also engages with collective memory—national, cultural, and historical—not through epic narration but through ethical absorption. Events of sacrifice, struggle, and loss are refracted through individual consciousness, foregrounding moral cost rather than heroic spectacle. In this respect, Ashodhiya's work aligns with a reflective poetic lineage that privileges questioning over certainty.

Language, Form, and Aesthetic Discipline

Ashodhiya's Hindi is marked by economy, idiomatic precision, and tonal balance. Drawing from spoken registers, regional inflections, and cultural metaphor, his diction remains accessible without lapsing into sentimentality. Structural features—pauses, silences, restrained metaphors—carry significant semantic weight. Absence functions as articulation; silence becomes meaning-bearing.

The English translations included in this volume represent a careful act of literary negotiation rather than literal substitution. The emphasis is on preserving tonal integrity, ethical nuance, and contemplative cadence. Where cultural concepts resist direct equivalence, their Indic resonance is intentionally retained, ensuring that the poems remain rooted even as they enter a translingual literary space. Translation, here, extends the inward journey rather than relocating it.

Antaryatrā as a Literary Project

Antaryatrā is not a casual assemblage of poems but a consciously structured literary project. The arrangement of texts follows an implicit emotional and philosophical progression—moving through devotion, doubt, fatigue, resistance, and quiet affirmation. Readers are invited not to consume the poems sequentially but to dwell within them, to pause, return, and recognize echoes of their own interior life.

In this sense, the collection participates in a lineage of Indian introspective writing while remaining distinctly contemporary. It responds to a cultural moment marked by speed, noise, and performativity through stillness, attentiveness, and ethical patience. The poems insist that inwardness is not withdrawal but resistance—to simplification, moral haste, and the erosion of interior life.

Conclusion: The Ethics of Inwardness

Ultimately, **Antaryatrā — The Inner Journey** affirms poetry's ethical responsibility to remain faithful to lived experience, even when that experience is unresolved, fatigued, or fragmented. Ashodhiya's poems do not offer easy reassurance; they offer recognition. They remind the reader that the most consequential journeys are often those undertaken without witnesses, applause, or certainty.

To read **Antaryatrā** is to accompany the poet inward—through silence, devotion, doubt, and measured resolve—and, in doing so, to rediscover one's own capacity for reflection. It is this shared inwardness, patiently and ethically articulated, that grants the collection its lasting literary and human significance.

Dr. Pushpa
Professor & Head
Department of Hindi
Maharshi Dayanand University, Rohtak

Literary–Critical Afterword

By K. Lal
(Krishna Lal, Retired Lecturer in English, Rohtak, Haryana)

Antaryātrā — *The Inner Journey*

1. The Poetics of Ethical Intimacy

Anand Kumar Ashodhiya's *Antaryātrā* occupies a significant and conscientious space in contemporary Hindi poetry—where the personal lyric does not withdraw from public responsibility, and moral awareness does not sacrifice emotional authenticity. His poetry transforms everyday lived experience into reflective utterance, allowing ordinary moments to carry ethical and philosophical weight.

The "inner journey" of *Antaryātrā* is not an escape into introspection alone; it is a sustained engagement with love, nationhood, social justice, faith, and silence as lived realities. These poems do not seek dramatic excess or rhetorical flourish. Instead, they move with restraint and clarity, inviting recognition rather than spectacle.

From the familial tenderness of poems like **"Father"** and **"The Granddaughter"** to the solemn national consciousness of **"Kargil Vijay Diwas — The Ballad of Kargil Glory"** and **"Shaheed-e-Azam Sardar Udham Singh,"** Ashodhiya's voice remains ethically grounded and emotionally sincere.

2. Language and Diction: Cultural Grounding

Ashodhiya's linguistic strength lies in his rootedness. His Hindi, shaped by regional cadence and cultural immediacy, achieves clarity without losing poetic gravity. The diction is lived rather than literary in the artificial sense—allowing poems such as **"Autobiography of a Ration-Depot Holder"** and **"Sir, They Call Me Gutkha!"** to sound authentic, urgent, and morally charged.

Even in English translation, the tonal honesty of the original survives. The poems retain their emotional register because they emerge from lived speech rather than ornamental abstraction. Language here is not performance; it is testimony.

3. Thematic Constellations

a. Love, Memory, and Emotional Restraint

In lyrical poems such as **"I Will Not Wear the Red Sari, O Beloved King," "The Soaked, Subtle Veil,"** and **"Beloved (Jaanam),"** love is portrayed not as romantic excess but as endurance shaped by memory, restraint, and dignity. Longing is tempered by silence; desire coexists with acceptance. These poems are elegiac without sentimentality, intimate without exhibition.

b. Patriotism as Moral Responsibility

Ashodhiya's patriotic poems resist sloganism. In works like **"Vijay Diwas — Victory Day," "Har Ghar Tiranga — The Tricolour at Every Home,"** and **"Constitution Day,"** nationalism is articulated as ethical commitment rather than emotional spectacle. Sacrifice is humanized, not glorified; nationhood emerges as duty anchored in conscience.

c. Social Witness and Protest

The poet's strongest moral urgency appears in poems such as **"Female Foeticide," "Why Should I Become Another Nirbhaya?"** and **"The Hunger in My Belly Won't Let Me Sleep."** These poems function as acts of witnessing—bringing marginal voices into poetic visibility. Ashodhiya avoids rhetorical anger; instead, his protest derives force from restraint and moral clarity.

d. Devotion and Philosophical Reflection

In poems like **"Sanātana Dharma — The Eternal Way," "SAVERA — The Dawn,"** and **"Time,"** spiritual reflection merges with ethical inquiry. Faith is not ritualistic; it is experiential and introspective. Silence, dawn, and temporality function as metaphors for inner discipline and moral awakening.

4. Imagery and Symbolic Economy

Ashodhiya's imagery is economical yet resonant.

- **Fire** signifies both transformation and sacrifice (as in "**Agniveers Shall Choose Their Fiery Path**").

- **Cloth, veil, and thread** evoke intimacy, memory, and vulnerability.

- **Silence** emerges repeatedly as a moral threshold—between speech and conscience, protest and restraint.

These symbols remain rooted in the tangible world while opening toward philosophical reflection.

5. Form, Rhythm, and Oral Sensibility

Though largely composed in free verse, Ashodhiya's poetry retains rhythmic coherence through repetition, cadence, and oral flow. Poems unfold with narrative clarity, echoing folk and conversational traditions. This orality ensures accessibility while maintaining lyrical discipline.

6. Evolution of Poetic Voice

Antaryātrā documents a discernible inward evolution:

- Early poems assert collective identity and national consciousness.

- Middle poems confront social injustice and ethical conflict.

- Later poems move toward philosophical quietude and introspection.

This progression reflects a deepening inward journey—from public declaration toward reflective moral solitude.

7. Distinctiveness and Literary Position

While Ashodhiya's ethical realism may invite comparison with socially engaged Hindi poets, his voice remains distinctly his own—shaped by regional grounding, emotional restraint, and moral attentiveness. In English translation, this sensibility survives, positioning him as a bridge between local experience and universal concern.

8. Conclusion: The Ethics of Lyric Responsibility

Through *Antaryātrā*, Anand Kumar Ashodhiya emerges as a poet of moral clarity and emotional restraint. His poetry neither retreats into private reverie nor surrenders to ideological noise. Instead, it inhabits the fragile space where feeling meets responsibility.

His poems do not shout; they endure. They remind us that poetry, at its truest, is not merely expression—it is conscience rendered audible.

K. Lal
(Krishna Lal, Retired Lecturer in English, Rohtak, Haryana)

Critical Appreciation

(From the Desk of the Editor-cum-Publisher: A Critical Appreciation)

The Poetic Vision of Anand Kumar Ashodhiya in *Antaryatrā — The Inner Journey*

Anand Kumar Ashodhiya's poetry unfolds across a wide emotional and ethical spectrum, engaging love and loss, dissent and devotion, social reality and inward reflection with equal seriousness. *Antaryatrā — The Inner Journey* is not merely a collection of poems but a sustained exploration of conscience—personal, collective, and spiritual. Each poem functions as an inward passage, affirming poetry as an act of awareness rather than ornamentation.

One of the defining strengths of Ashodhiya's work lies in his fearless engagement with lived reality. In poems such as *Danga* (Parts I & II) and *Kargil*, the poet confronts violence, history, and sacrifice not through abstraction but through ethical immediacy. *Danga* stands as a stark witness to communal rupture, where the poet speaks from within the devastation, allowing moral anguish to replace rhetoric. In *Kargil*, patriotism is rendered as disciplined reverence rather than spectacle; martyrdom becomes a symbol of collective moral courage, stripped of sentimentality.

Equally compelling is Ashodhiya's treatment of love and loss. His lyrical poems do not romanticize emotion; instead, they trace the quiet aftershocks of intimacy, separation, and remembrance. Longing, in his verse, is neither indulgent nor theatrical—it is restrained, reflective, and deeply human. Personal grief expands into universal resonance, allowing private experience to assume metaphysical depth.

Ashodhiya's social vision emerges with particular force in poems addressing hypocrisy, systemic injustice, and moral erosion. His critique is grounded in empathy rather than accusation. Using irony, realism, and understated satire, he exposes the fractures of contemporary life while preserving the dignity of the human subject. The poet's voice here is that of a moral witness—alert, compassionate, and unafraid to disturb complacency.

The spiritual dimension of *Antaryatrā* does not rely on doctrinal assertion. Instead, it unfolds through silence, restraint, and inward questioning. Poems centered on stillness and self-examination transform reflection into a form of ethical discipline. Faith appears as lived inquiry rather than proclamation, aligning devotion with moral clarity and humility.

Stylistically, Ashodhiya's language bridges the earthiness of regional idiom with the grace of literary Hindi, retaining musicality even in free verse. His diction is unadorned yet resonant, capable of carrying both folk immediacy and philosophical weight. In English translation, this voice retains its moral lyricism, extending the poet's inward journey to a broader readership without diluting its cultural interiority.

In sum, Anand Kumar Ashodhiya emerges in *Antaryatrā — The Inner Journey* as a poet of ethical depth and emotional restraint. His poetry does not seek applause; it seeks recognition. It stands as a reminder that the most enduring literary journeys are those undertaken quietly—through reflection, responsibility, and compassion. This collection affirms poetry's enduring role as the conscience of its time, articulated with humility, courage, and inward light.

— *Editor-cum-Publisher*
Avikavani Publishers

About the Translator: Anand Kumar Ashodhiya

Anand Kumar Ashodhiya—known in the Haryanvi literary world as *Kavi Anand Shahpur*—brings together disciplined service, linguistic finesse, and deep cultural rootedness.

A former Warrant Officer of the Indian Air Force, he served for thirty-two years with distinction and was honoured for his contribution to **Rajbhasha Hindi**. Holding a postgraduate degree in English Literature from Annamalai University, he is well equipped to bridge linguistic and cultural sensibilities between Hindi–Haryanvi and English.

Deeply anchored in the ethos of Haryana, his literary name honours his ancestral village, **Shahpur Turk (Sonipat, Haryana)**. With **over 380 compositions** spanning dohā, geet, ghazal, short stories, and folk-poetic traditions, he is recognised for his mastery of regional idiom, metre, and narrative expression—qualities that make him uniquely suited to translate his own Hindi poems into English.

Literary Contributions

His diverse oeuvre includes:

- *Adhirājan* — Folk epic in Ragni form First and Second Volume
- *Thara Mudda Thari Baat* — Modern Haryanvi poems
- *Kissa Bhagat Puranmal* — Ragni with Pingal Samiksha
- *Heer Ranjha* — Ragni with Pingal Samiksha
- *Avikāvani Haryanvi Ragni Sangrah* (with Samiksha)
- *Draupadi: A Folk Consciousness* — Ragni Sangrah with Samiksha
- *Prem ke Sau Rang* — Modern Hindi poems
- *Sākēt: An English Trans-creation*
- *NISWARTHI UDYOGA PARVA: An English Translation*
- *Kahaan Kahaan Paiband Lagau — An English Translation*
- *Ath Marjarika Uvaach (Grand Epic: The Great Battle of Indian History)* [Symbolic Rereading: From the Beginning to 2025]
- And the present volume, *Antaryātrā — The Inner Journey: An English Transliteration*

Born on **1 April** in Shahpur Turk, Haryana, and presently residing in Mumbai, he continues to write actively across languages and genres.

Honours and Recognitions

Recipient of several cultural and literary distinctions—including the **Haryana Sanskriti Gaurav Ratna**, **Kargil Vijay Samman**, and

Haryanvi Sahitya Ratna 2025—Ashodhiya remains committed to bringing Indian vernacular and classical literary traditions to a wider global readership.